Coconut Wireless Life

A GUIDEBOOK

Kim Pierce

The Larry Czerwonka Company, LLC
Hilo, Hawai'i

20% of the proceeds from this book are being donated
to programs for Big Island youth.

Note to traveler:

Go get a pen.

You are going to want to
write in this book!

First Edition — November 2014

This book is set in 12-point Garamond

Published by: The Larry Czerwonka Company, LLC
http://thelarryczerwonkacompany.com

Cover design and illustrations by Brooke Nelson

Printed in the United States of America

ISBN: 0692323503
ISBN-13: 978-0692323502

*This guidebook is dedicated to
Max and to Cooper. Two special teachers.*

*And to Keith Kochner who taught me the
importance of seeking mentors and then trained
me how to do it.*

*A special thank you to Julie and Grif,
you have changed my life.*

*I realize as a young adult that I was blessed to be
raised by parents who also qualify as mentors. Of
course, I haven't always seen them as such, but
truly my parents are my first examples and for
those examples I am grateful.
I love you both very much.*

You know the expression S.O.B? (Son of a Bitch)

Well, on the Big Island of Hawai'i the expression is F.O.B. It means Fresh Off the Boat. Like when you come from somewhere else and you just show up. You are fresh off the boat.

Despite the postcard perfect palms, crystal blue waves and incredible island culture that is Hawai'i, when you are FOB . . . life is just going to be a little rougher for a while. Most people who come here don't stay. And everyone knows it, so people, employers, and landlords behave accordingly. In the summer of 2004, I had packed my books and bikinis and followed my boyfriend to the Big Island. I was F.O.B. and 100% stoked to be in Hawai'i. With zero contacts except for said boyfriend and his three dorky friends who only want to talk about scuba diving, I rolled up my fresh and expensive graduate degree and began my career in Hawai'i slinging noodles at the restaurant down the street because graduate degree or not—no one hires F.O.B's. I went from an environment where most things made sense or followed a logical flow, to an Island where almost all of the rules are different. Not good, not bad, but different. Real different.

It was clear that the rules had changed when I was sitting in the waiting room at the community health clinic one afternoon. A woman was across the way with her grandchildren. Everyone had been in there too long and it was hot, everyone was sick of waiting including her grandkids. My name got called to go in. She looked me dead in the eyes and said, "fucking *Haole*." She was pissed. She was pissed because of what I represented to her—and that is an opportunity to look inside. Look up *Haole*. It's a commonly used term now, but it certainly didn't originate as a compliment. This instance in the waiting room was the perfect punch in the face. Here, on this incredible island, all the rules were different.

It was clear. My environment changed so quickly and drastically I was going to either retaliate in anger, attempting to hold on to all that I knew before, or just keep taking the punches and adjust from the inside out. It was me, who was going to adjust. Not the environment. From the inside out. After one year on this special Island, I knew I would rather live in a tent under a bridge still figuring it out, then go back to what I used to know as normal. Normal felt uninspiring. Hawai'i felt spectacular, brutal and life changing. And it has been.

My Coconut Wireless Life (CWL)

This guidebook, *Coconut Wireless Life*, is a compilation of teachings. Offerings that I give to you because they are helpful for anyone who wants to create an amazing life. The Big Island beauty and people motivated me to create a LIFE BY DESIGN. I wanted to surf when the waves were good, work hard at projects I am passionate about, all with a backdrop of this unbelievable island full of incredible people.

Now here is the special part—the Coconut Wireless is real, but you can't see it. When you chew on, barf up, then digest these teachings again, you will find that the people and resources you are looking for are ALL AROUND. But to get connected the work must come from the inside out. You adapt first, then everything else follows. Hawaiians seem to inherently know this. A people connected to nature and each other. Island living intensifies connection. It's hot here . . . and it's awesome.

Here is the deal. I'm an over-achiever. The cool part was that LITTLE OF THIS COUNTED when I moved to Hawai'i. I was forced to grow a bunch of other stuff, inside. Here is my outside overachiever list: Born into a family of privilege and responsibility. We never had the nicest stuff, but we always had what we needed and more. My parents set up situations for us to earn it. BA University of Arizona and Division One athlete—Bear Down. I completed a three year graduate program (in two years) at Santa Clara University in Counseling Psychology. I learned more there in two years than all of my education prior combined. Moved to Big Island in 2004.

Here in Hawai'i, I run a network marketing business with Arbonne International, from my hammock. I write. I attempt to garden and I am a founding member of the Hilo Health Cooperative. For fun, I want to be around the ocean. To be of service I am a licensed Marriage and Family Therapist in California and Hawai'i.

I'm most happy hanging out with my family and friends cruising this sweet, sweet island.

Legend

Island Love: This icon represents some of the nuggets of greatness that I have managed to collect in my time on this incredible rock. Hawai'i is a remarkable place. It is no wonder so much grows here. Including me. The longer I stay, the less I know.

Movies: My husband loves movies and makes the best popcorn. You can learn so much from what you choose to watch. These movies are the good ones.

Links: This will all be good stuff to poke around on when you are killing time at work. Stop Facebooking and do a little homework. Check out these links.

OPD's: This one's for my mom. Opportunity for Personal Development, think of them like mini challenges. These are designed to be fun. Challenges like floating in water, oil pulling and donating clothes. Nothing that's gonna kill you, but everything that is good for you. Coconut Wireless Life is a journey. Plan to sweat.

Books: I might be considered a voracious reader. I'm not sure the official number that qualifies someone for that title. I bet I'm on the edge. I'm focused and often I focus on books and then applying what I learn. These are my books. The short list. Nothing made it on here that you should skip. You could work from the list for a lifetime. You would also probably begin to levitate. Just a warning. You're welcome.

Music. I was musically deprived as a child, and this is my attempt at a comeback. Good music is essential to have around. These are some of my favorites.

HABITS
+
MINDSET
+
SERVICE
+
MENTORS
=
CWL

Steamroller

You ever watch a steamroller do its thing? The function is not really to roll things over per se, but more to press down into the foundation. A layer is put down and the steam roller presses it down with enormous weight and pressure.

You want to do that for yourself with these lessons and create habits. Take the time to press them down in yourself. It's why this text should be with you and around you for as long as you see fit. It's a really good way to make sure the teachings have a chance to get pressed into your foundation. Put this guide in your gym bag or purse. Take it to the beach and on vacation. Travel with it. Be in motion together for some time.

Today's date is _____

Six months from now will be _____

Most people do too much. They read too much, try to learn too much, commit to too much and absorb absolutely nothing. Nothing sticks because they haven't protected quality time with any ONE thing. Don't waste that kind of energy. 😌

I know you can read this book in two nights, but keep it on hand for the next six months. Steamroller.

Habits

Here is something I know for sure: *stoked* people (feeling joy and working with a sense of purpose) are the ones who can find the space between behavior and emotion. What I mean is that they are, in fact, separate. Behavior is the action that you repeatedly do. Emotion is how you feel about yourself and then your external world. When you find the space between behaviors and emotions, you can make the decision to do certain behaviors whether or not you feel like it at any given moment. This is a really big idea. Most people are so consumed by their current emotional state that it dictates everything, including all their behaviors.

The habit section of this book comes first because it will put you into motion. Commit to these habits. Don't worry about whether you feel like it or not. Depending on the day, you may or may not. Just focus on the habits. Study and practice these habits. Whether you are feeling happy, sad, capable, freaked out or completely apathetic, just begin to apply yourself to these habits and you will be rolling. Everything else will FLOW.

Successful people have rough days all the time. The difference is that they find the space between their current emotion and the behaviors they know to do. Become that way. It's the first part of the journey. Get your ass out of park and in gear. Practice the habits, we are beginning the journey.

▶ Here are some EXCELLENT movies:

- *Bustin' Down the Door*
- *FLOW*
- *Office Space*
- *Happy*
- *Avatar*
- *What the Bleep Do We Know?*
- *Cinderella Man*
- *Dirt!*
- *Fed Up*
- *180° South*

You Run the Day

Either you run the day or the day runs you.
— JIM ROHN

You gotta, gotta, gotta make a plan. You just have to. So make a game plan for your day. What is wonderful about having a plan is that it's just a backbone. You can add or take away or change or abandon ship when you need to (I wrote this book with a child under the age of two, I completely understand abandon ship). When you have a plan, all of your decisions about what to change are better because there has been conscious thought about it. The idea is to eliminate the willie-nillie, non-focused, daze time. Don't confuse this with enjoying times of re-laxation. Just make sure you are enjoying relaxation time because you intended it, planned for it . . . not just because you ended up there due to lack of focus.

Those who fail to plan, basically plan to fail. So the night before, identify the two or three most important things you want to complete the next day. It's that simple. On a post it note, on your cell phone. However you want to do it, have it ready to go when you wake. The three most important things you can do tomorrow. Simple.

How you live your day is in fact how you live your life..

The best 3 things for me to do tomorrow:

1. _____

2. _____

3. _____

Be A NINJA

When you adhere yourself to this one single principle, you will at least be on the right form of nutrition. Your mind is basically a computer. So you MUST, MUST, MUST spend a minimum of 30 minutes a day digesting good nutrition for your mind. You eat every day to nourish your body. Do the same for your mind. 30 minutes a day on the intake of good nutrition for your mind is required to pull off your *COCONUT WIRELESS LIFE*. Make it simple and conducive to your lifestyle. Reading books, being selective about the movies you watch, listening to audio tracks while you drive will get you 30 minutes easy. But it must be something every day for 30 minutes. Even if you have to break it up into 10 minute chunks.

For some, 30 minutes a day may feel like a chore to start. Others of you will jump right in and find it easy. Spending time with this text counts towards your 30 minutes each day.

This habit once planted will grow into a passion and a lifestyle. And whatever you were passionate and good at before, you will just get better. My friend and I call developing this habit "ninja training."

30 minutes a day, no matter what. Be a ninja.

The Slight Edge by Jeff Olsen

Show Up

There is always that meeting, that appointment, that commitment, the gym or a practice that we know we should go to. For me, it usually happens in the afternoon. When I would rather not go, but I know that I SHOULD go. JUST GET YOURSELF THERE. I have found that if I take all the pressure off myself in terms of how the meeting/appointment will go and just focus on getting myself there. The rest takes care of itself. So take the pressure off, and just commit to getting your butt out the door.

That is really the only part that takes your own effort. Once you are there, the energy you need, the motivation, the focus and the people you are supposed to be around will all be present. You just have to get yourself there. None of this will be available unless you show up.

You must show up.

Hard work pays off in the future, laziness pays off now.
— STEVEN WRIGHT

Gratitude

Like everyone else on the planet, I have off days. During these days, I force myself to write down the things that I am grateful for. A roof over my head, food, a car that runs, a healthy family. I just write them down. If you have these things I mentioned, you have it better than the vast majority of the planet, so get grateful. On the days that you don't FEEL like taking the time to make a gratitude list, *DO IT*, because those are the days it is most important. Make a list mentally while driving, or even better, write it down. This habit will completely change the flow of your energy and your day. Live in gratitude, seek it, share it and condition your body, mind and heart to run on the energy of gratitude.

Gratitude suffocates Negativity. Some people could stand to paint this on the wall of their home or office. It is so essential that you cultivate a sense of gratitude. Depending on your temperament, some people find this easier than others. There is a discipline associated with training yourself to recognize all that you have to be grateful for, especially when you don't feel like it at all!

F.U.E.L.: Focused-Unlimited-Extraordinary-Life by Trisha L. Moore

 Songs that help with gratitude:

- "Mitakuye Oyasin" – Nahko and Medicine for the People.
- "Good Rain" – Trevor Hall

 Make a gratitude list. No directions. Just make one. Scratch paper or use the *F.U.E.L Journal*

Do Less

Most people are OVER COMMITTED. I mean that we are in too many clubs, volunteering for too many things, on one too many committees, doing too much at work. Just like an octopus on roller skates. Lots of good intention but when you really look at what's happening, it's a directionless exhausting mess. In addition, the results in an over-committed life will be mediocre at best! You must allow the time and focus for excellence. So here is the challenge: Say NO to EVERYTHING, I mean EVERYTHING. Nothing new what-so-ever until your time with this book is complete. Some of you will say "That's impossible!, I could never do that." Yes, you can. Don't be ridiculous! I did it. You can do it. Many *AKAMAI* economists and philosophers have proven that 80% of our outcomes are generated from 20% of our efforts. ACROSS THE BOARD. This includes you. So start saying: "No thank you," "Now isn't the right time" or "Check with me in six months." Begin to enjoy the view as your life CLEARS UP. This is an awesome and necessary process to get excellent at anything. Take off the roller skates!

 Commit to NOTHING NEW for four months.

 Akamai (Hawaiian word for smart, intelligent.)

- *The 4-Hour Workweek* by Timothy Ferriss
- *Launching a Leadership Revolution* by Chris Brady and Oorwin Woodward
- *Do Less, Be More* by John Busacker

Masterminds

You are the average of the 5 people
you spend the most time with.
— JIM ROHN

You are going to want to take *at least a week* as you absorb this concept. You could stay on this page for seven days. SIT with that for a moment. You are the sum of the five you spend the most time with. The average health, average happiness, average wealth, education blah blah blah blah blah . . . of the five people you hang around with the most. Period. So here is a hint: BE SELECTIVE.

Love people where they are at. This has nothing to do with judging others. Once you understand the power that those around you have you MUST be wise with your time and your focus and honor it enough to spend it with those who inspire you, challenge you, push you and teach you.

Take an inventory this week of who you are with the most. Check out the "favorites" in your cell phone and start to consider if shifts need to happen in your top five.

Growing up, I fantasized with a friend about being in the Mafia. Mafia: a powerful and influential group within an organization. Your masterminds are your mafia.

 Delete the favorites list in your cell phone and redo it after thirty days.

 mentorfish.com

Want to meet some of my Masterminds? Check 'em out at coconutwirelesslife.com and say Aloha to Brooke, Asia, Heather and Annie.

Toastmasters

It's this simple. Creating habits of successful people is easy when you have something to show up to. Ha ha! Sound familiar? Toastmasters is just that, an organization that throws you outside of your comfort zone and encourages you to grow. You can put it on your resume and you can go on your lunch break from work. There isn't a lot to talk about. Just start going. Ask a friend to go with you. Find someone who looks nice and sit next to them. You can find your local chapter on-line.

Remember how we talked about Ninja Training? This would count for personal development every time you attend a meeting.

See you there.

> We learn best in moments of enjoyment.
> — RALPH SMEDLEY (Founder of Toastmasters)

 SPEAK (Toastmasters documentary)

 toastmasters.org

 www.HiloToastmasters.com (Club #248)

Super Duper Computer Head

This is such a big deal and a personal passion of mine. I considered running this chapter back to back 3x and then sprinkling it in a few other times before the end of the text. Read, Re-read and memorize this concept. You might consider a tattoo with some saying to help you remember how essential this habit is for creating success in your life.

Your mind is basically a computer. It simply does what you tell it. When you ruminate, daydream and talk to yourself (which we ALL do WAY more than we realize) your computer is on and following instructions that you are giving it.

When we say negative, nasty things to ourselves, our computer files what we said and operates from those directions. Most people say negative and mean comments to themselves that they would NEVER even consider saying to another person! We are often our most harsh critic and that results in some really brutal and intense negative programming on our computer.

Train this habit and allow for neural rewiring in order to get more stoked. Let this concept work to your advantage and gain you momentum. *You must be your own superfan* and get your supercomputer of a noggin to work for you. Take control of the programming. Use the words and thoughts you have about yourself to your advantage. Make them positive. This phenomenon can actually be mapped out neurologically and we can see changes in brain circuitry. It's the same as if a gardener was choosing which plants to water and which ones to not water.

We grow new roots and connections in our minds just like the roots of a plant grows when watered. The best way to water the roots you want to grow in your mind? Pay attention to your own LANGUAGE.

From my perspective, the focused human mind is the most powerful instrument in the universe, and thru the use of language, our left brain is capable of directing (or impeding) our physical healing and recovery. My verbal left ego mind functions as head cheerleader of my fifty trillion molecular geniuses and when I periodically encourage my cells with "you go girls!" I can't help but think this induces some sort of vibration within my body that promotes a healing environment.
— DR. JILL BOLTE TAYLOR

- *The Power of Neuroplasticity* by Shad Helmstetter, Ph.D.
- *Hardwiring Happiness* and *Buddha's Brain* by Rick Hanson, Ph.D.
- *My Stroke of Insight* by Jill Bolte Taylor, Ph.D.
- *Excuses Begone* by Dr. Wayne W. Dyer

Dr. Helmstetter and me (Fall 2012)

Language

LANGUAGE is foundational as you create your *COCONUT WIRELESS LIFE.*

The easiest and quickest way to get your super computer brain functioning in your favor is to monitor your language. Here are some simple guidelines to implement yesterday: ☺

- ✓ Only talk about what you DO want. Spend ZERO time talking about what you don't want.
- ✓ Only speak in the direction of your own greatness and the greatness of others. This instantly eliminates gossip and back talking.
- ✓ Bring to a halt the private thoughts we use to beat ourselves up. Recognize them for what they are and just set them down for a time. You are watering new roots and connections. Set the other stuff down.
- ✓ Stay persistent about this habit. It's exactly the same as building muscle. You need to build this habit up over time. NEVER STOP . . . it keeps getting better.
- ✓ Get support. Check out EVERYTHING written and recorded by Dr. Shad Helmstetter, especially the *Self-Talk* CD's for kids and adults.
- ✓ Ask someone to hold you accountable. Someone you trust who is willing to let you know if you aren't following these guidelines, or even better, high five you when you are following them. Someone who could help me with this would be:

Meditate

There is no right or wrong way to meditate, so just start somewhere.

Spiritually, I think it all begins here. Developing (yes, it takes development) a regular habit of spending time by yourself quietly is essential for human well-being. As more people begin to do this more often, you see the impact. We are in a global relations CRISIS, mostly embedded in the fact that the average person can't stand to be alone in a room by himself for very long.

Meditation is hard, intense, and wonderful and there are hundreds of ways to do it. Just find what works for you. You will be DOING LESS, so carving out 10 minutes to begin a meditation practice will be simple. Find a time and find a place and just begin. This habit will serve you forever.

By meditation we mean something very basic and simple that is not tied to any one culture. We are talking about a very basic and simple act: sitting on the ground, assuming a good' posture, and developing a sense of our spot, our place on this earth. This is the means of re-discovering our basic goodness, the means to tune ourselves in to genuine reality, without any expectation or preconceptions.

— Chögyam Trungpa Rinpoche

- *Getting in the Gap* by Dr. Wayne W. Dyer (Book with audio to help)
- *Shambhala: The Sacred Path of the Warrior* by Chögyam Trungpa Rinpoche

Doing Time, Doing Vipassana

 Malie (Hawaiian word used to describe the ocean. A serene and calm ocean. No waves, just a smooth ocean. I use this image when I meditate.)

HABITS
+
MINDSET
+
SERVICE
+
MENTORS
=
CWL

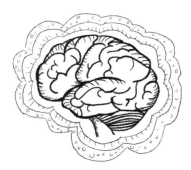

Empires of the Mind

The empires of the future are the empires of the mind.
— WINSTON CHURCHILL

As your daily habits begin to take shape, your mind will rewire to support those changes: Habits *1ˢᵗ*, Mindset *2ᴺᴰ*.

HABITS+MINDSET+SERVICE+MENTORS=CWL

So far, so good. HABITS. Now MINDSET. Keep it up.

Your mind is the most powerful tool you have to help you change everything about your current circumstance. Your mind can be your greatest ally and your worst enemy, so honor the power of your mind as you dip into some high-octane learning.

It's your life . . . it's worth being on purpose with your thoughts, because your thoughts create your life.

    Launching a Leadership Revolution
by Chris Brady and Orrin Woodward

To have a high quality of life,
we must have a high quality of thought.
There is power in belief, it is fact that beliefs control realities.

    A Return to Love by Marianne Williamson

An untrained mind can accomplish nothing.

23

Money Money Money

This has become a favorite topic of mine. Mostly because the messages around money usually include, "Don't talk about it" or "It's rude to ask." I have come to understand money as one form of energy. Just **ONE** form of energy but an important and powerful one.

What is your self-talk around your finances?

Bob Proctor says, "If you want to do good in this world, get rich first." He goes on to say, "Money serves two purposes so get it straight: 1. Money can make you comfortable. 2. Money can extend the scope of your services beyond your physical presence. The good you can do without money will be severely limited."

Here is something else that will REALLY help with your mindset around money:

Stop paying attention to the Joneses. Less really is more. I promise you don't need new houses, cars, and all that STUFF. It's just stuff. Keep your living expenses low (families studied with the happiest quality of life in the U.S. have incomes of 75K/year) and then earn a lot of money so you can do good work with it.

There is a natural law of abundance which pervades
the entire universe, but it will not flow through a doorway
of belief in lack and limitation.
— PAUL ZAITER

Pay attention to the feeling state you are in, your private thoughts when you are spending money. Some purchases feel wonderful, others feel energetically lower. Pay attention to that, and use it as a guide. We vote with our dollar so vote for what you want to see more of.

 Mind altering books about Money:

- *The Soul of Money* by Lynne Twist
- *The Diamond Cutter* by Geshe Michael Roach
- *You Were Born Rich* by Bob Proctor

http://bit.ly/happy75K "The Perfect Salary for Happiness"

Distraction

Don't be distracted by others' lack of goals or focus.

Most people don't think past the end of the day. You are going to start thinking with a much longer vision in mind. CWL includes long range vision planning, so you must be the one prepared to utilize your mind and energy wisely to support YOUR big dreams. I always have a backup activity planned, even if it is sitting quietly and meditating. Most people are late, get lost, forget or aren't prepared for meetings or appointments. Because of this, I always have a backup activity. It honors the high value of my time. If there is a mess-up or miscommunication it's no problem, because I have prepared my mind and have prepared a backup plan.

I AM responsible for my focus and use of time, not other people.

You adapt. You must be the one to adapt your thinking and your habits around everyone else.

It is very easy to get dizzy and distracted in a world with infinite stimulus. Presently your culture and environment are probably not working in your favor. We have created an environment of constant distraction. You must learn about and cultivate your ability to focus. Train your mind to stay focused in a culture that is more cluttered with non-sense than ever before.

#1 reason people don't get their goals is due to broken focus.
— KEITH KOCHNER

🏆 ZERO gossip/smut magazines. Zero. Just drop them from your life. They don't serve you. Just to be clear, anything in the grocery store checkout line is a smut magazine.

Limit your time on Facebook to 10 minutes a day. Send messages to your friends and then SIGN OFF!

♫ "There is no medicine on television. Turn it off, and turn yourself around." – from "Manifesto" by Medicine for the People

Things I do each day that help me get to where I want to be:

_____

_____

_____

_____

Things I do each day that are just filler or distraction:

_____

_____

_____

Thinkin' About Thinkin' About

It does not matter what other people think. Almost all of the time.

I realize that at first glimpse, this may sound brutal and self-centered.

That's okay. Here are some concepts I would ask you to consider.

> Have you heard the expression, "They say"?
> Have you ever asked yourself who *they* are anyway?
> And have you noticed that *they* are always
> changing their thinking?
> — KEITH KOCHNER

It's necessary to stop caring what other people think unless they are your MENTORS and are supporting your greatness. This means at times you will have to make a conscious decision to ignore the opinions of family and close friends. The voice in your head that guides your own sense of purpose must be louder than the voices from outside. Some people exist to criticize. If they stopped criticizing, they would cease to exist. So just remove yourself from their environment. Close your office door, take them out of your speed dial, think *earmuffs*. Do whatever you have to do to protect your focus and attention on what you DO WANT. All your mental focus needs to be on what you DO WANT and where you ARE GOING. People stuck in complaining or criticizing mode will just simply rotate people to talk about . . . so find your way out of that rotation. It's one of the biggest favors you can do for yourself and it is essential as you create your own CWL.

As you go about life leading with your heart, defaulting to love and creating your future, I promise you are going to piss a few people off.

Plan on it. Adjust to it. Smile and be nice and just factor it in as part of the journey. Some get it, some don't, so what, carry on.

> We are a product of the books we read, the things
> we listen to and the people we associate with.
> — CHRIS BRADY and OORWIN WOODWARD
> (Launching a Leadership Revolution)

'Olu'olu (Hawaiian word meaning pleasant, to have a pleasing manner with friendly overtones, ego-free.) A mentor reminded me that all I can control is my own behavior. Not others responses. So do your best to stay *'olu'olu*.

Activity Not Outcome

WARNING . . . when you understand this concept and live by it not only will it save your life and I am certain it's the road to greater spirituality, whatever that means for you.

An example: Did you know that there is no end game in yoga? If you are holding too tightly to the desire for perfection, you will never get there with the poses. The practice and spiritual evolution of yoga comes from the decision to keep getting on your mat. Again and again and again.

This mentality can be the same for all areas of your life. You will do your best and perform at your highest when you have attached your feeling to *doing the activity* and not the *outcome of the activity*. See the difference? There comes a time when you fall in love with the regular and seemingly mundane miracles in your daily life. This is a gift.

 Light on Yoga and *Light on Life* by B.K.S. Iyengar

You Matter

When one man, for whatever reason,
has the opportunity to lead an extraordinary life,
he has no right to keep it to himself.
— JACQUES YVES COUSTEAU

This is high octane and vitally important. Our society and our planet are in a situation where more people need to do better. PERIOD. The *norm* must improve. That is my personal opinion and perhaps this is something you have also considered.

You got your hands on this book for a reason. So make these lessons **MOVE** and become a part of your life. We are short on people who are truly making a difference in the community around them. Most people are too *busy*, well so are the ants. You are tasked to become one of them if you have this guidebook. My guess is that you are creating your *COCONUT WIRELESS LIFE* so you can have more time to do the things you are passionate about and to be of service. So much improves in your own life when you can be of service to others

Training your mind is required in the journey.

Carry on.

Learning to value and utilize all of our cognitive
gifts opens our lives up to the masterpiece of life we
truly are. Imagine the compassionate world we could
create if we set our mind to it.
— DR. JILL BOLTE TAYLOR

Opportunity: It Can Hide

Don't miss it because it doesn't look the way you thought it would.

A mentor told me that most people create results around wanting to be right, not necessarily successful.

Did you hear what I said?! This is such a big deal . . . What are you dying to be right about?

In HABITS, we talked about doing less and meditating and by cultivating these two habits you will find that you actually have more mental capacity and energy available. It's really wonderful when you start to feel this happen. As the clutter of your mind and your life begin to clear up you will realize that most of what you need is already around you. For example, I got turned down for a meeting, but two weeks later was with the exact same group of people for a different event. I was able to enjoy that event and reap the benefits of being with those people because I didn't get hung up on having it go my way with the initial meeting two weeks prior. In fact, what you will find is that when you loosen your grip and release your need to be right, often what bubbles up is even better. That meeting massively upgraded into a girls' evening, sipping wine, in a hot tub overlooking all of Hilo Bay on the Big Island of Hawai'i. I would have completely missed the opportunity if I had forced that first meeting based on my own need to be right.

It's All Here

As your mind sharpens itself, you will realize that you have most of what you need already around you. Often a project that you are working on will also work for something else with a similar purpose. Be aware of the temptation to fill in the negative space of your mind and life with clutter. KEEP IT CLEAR. It will take a concerted effort to keep it clear and it's well worth it. This space will help you see how much abundance and energetic alignment is already happening in your life. You will start to experience the feeling of moving with the current rather than against it. Your efforts become less forced and you gain more traction.

theminimalists.com

 Minimalism: A Documentary

 When you realize you need to buy something, just wait a few days. See if what you need shows up. I've manifested coffee mugs, office supplies, furniture, clothes. It's incredible. Just wait a few days before purchasing, and see what shows up.

This isn't a new concept. Like the recording artist Pete Seeger? Check out what he has to say about getting it done with less in his song "If It Can't Be Reduced."

Efficient vs. Effective

Efficiency is performing a given task (whether important or not) in the most economical manner possible.

Effectiveness is doing the tasks that get you closer to your goals.

In *The 4-Hour Workweek*, Timothy Ferriss wrote, "Being efficient without regard to effectiveness is the default mode of the universe." Thank you Mr. Ferriss! I don't need to add anything. Please THINK about how importance this difference is.

If that that felt like a punch in the face, apologies, just want to make sure you are paying attention. 😌

 The 4-Hour Workweek by Timothy Ferriss (I studied this book for six months solid and it still remains on the top of my pile. I consider it a textbook. I would have named it "ROCKING Life 101.")

fourhourworkweek.com

REVIEW

Take some time to review and think about how much of HABITS and MINDSET you have truly begun to absorb. This type of personal development work becomes a lifestyle, so do yourself a favor and review, revisit, contemplate and continue to digest these sections before moving on. It's the same as you would do for a really great meal or glass of wine. Eat it slowly, enjoy the taste. Do that with the first two sections for at least **one week** and longer if you would like.

To appreciate the payoff of SERVICE and MENTORS, you must have a cellular feeling about the lessons we've covered so far. Your body, mind and heart need to be in alignment with these teachings so you can maximize the rest of the guidebook. Arriving Destination Awesome. I've included a review if it helps.

You will be so happy you took the time to review. It will make the SERVICE and MENTOR sections feel SUPERSIZED—and not in the creepy McDonalds way.

Take this book to the beach (or your happy place) and see you in one week.

Which of the habits are things you are already doing?

_____

_____

Do some of them come naturally?

_____

_____

Which are ones you totally need to work on?

_____

_____

Who is Shad Helmstetter?

_____

_____

☐ Have you checked out Toastmasters?

🏆 Which of the OPD challenges did you test out?

_____

_____

☐ Did you try clearing your cell phone favorites list?—scary I know!

☐ How about making a gratitude list. Any attempts?

Which movies have you been watching lately?

_____

_____

Are you buying silly magazines that don't serve your greatness? Or reading enriching books? Which ones?

_____

_____

☐ Did you ask someone to hold you accountable for your language like we talked about on page 17? Who?

_____

This review is just a chance to check-in. No one knows but you.

So check-in. Your *COCONUT WIRELESS LIFE* is there. Right there, it's just small shifts.

Do this work and everything changes.

See you in SERVICE. It's a big one.

HABITS
+
MINDSET
+
SERVICE
+
MENTORS
=
CWL

Service and Gratitude

Being of service is easy when you begin with gratitude. SERVICE is step three in our CWL equation. You MUST BE OF SERVICE. Sometimes things go your way. Other times they do not. At least you don't think so at the time. Reorganize your mind to be grateful REGARDLESS of present circumstance. Conditioning yourself to be of service will increase the access you get with Mentors. Be of service. Period. Be of service to mentors to increase your access to them. Let's practice being of service and being grateful together.

This is a high-value activity.

It can feel like a discipline at times. There are days when practicing the habit of sitting down and simply writing a list of the things I am grateful for will CHANGE EVERYTHING. It will be the most important task I do that day. I have found this is an extremely valuable exercise and habit to cultivate. I needed structure to begin building this practice. I used a specific journal and began making a gratitude list 1x/week. Monday mornings, I would spend 20 minutes listing the things I was grateful for. We now have science that proves this type of activity changes the neural circuitry of your brain. It's like going to the gym for your mind.

 Man's Search for Meaning by Viktor E. Frankl

the last of human freedoms—to choose one's attitude
in any given set of circumstances, to choose one's own way.

This is your CREATIVE, BE OF SERVICE, FEEL GOOD, HAVE FUN AND TAKE NOTES SECTION:

In these open pages, you will find quotes about the importance of service and some ideas to start. Use this space to make notes about what you are *grateful* for, and to reflect on how you are being of *service*. There is no right or wrong way to do this. Intentional acts of kindness will take you very far in life. Make notes and capture your thoughts about what you like, your dreams, how to be of service and gratitude.

buy someone flowers

Be of service, be a sensible person.
— NAHKO and MEDICINE FOR THE PEOPLE

donate clothes

I believe that all greatness on some level is linked to service.
— KEITH KOCHNER

make a special meal for someone

leave a big tip at a restaurant

Make service a part of your beingness.
— KEITH KOCHNER

43

Serving is not an event. It's a lifestyle.
— KEITH KOCHNER

take a friend to yoga for the first time

volunteer for a cause

To open doors in relationships lead with serving.
— KEITH KOCHNER

give food from your yard to friends

The best way to find yourself is to lose yourself
in the service of others.
— MAHATMA GANDHI

buy a friend lunch

The Simple Path
Silence is Prayer
Prayer is Faith
Faith is Love
Love is Service
The Fruit of Service is Peace.
— MOTHER TERESA

make and drop off a meal at a friend's house

offer to give a ride

How may I serve?
— DR. WAYNE W. DYER

purchase a fundraiser ticket

Synonyms for service: favor, kindness, good turn, helping hand

help a friend grocery shop

invite a friend over for a meal

research a topic online for a friend

serv•ice
'sərvis/
noun: service
the action of helping or doing work for someone.

volunteer for a fundraiser

HABITS
+
MINDSET
+
SERVICE
+
MENTORS
=
CWL

Mentors

Have you ever gone on a really important trip? I mean a journey, a real adventure, where you need to be thoughtful about what you packed? Embarking on a journey of seeking out mentors should have the same feel about it. Thoughtful, planned and with plenty of preparation in advance. Take some inventory before you advance into this final phase. You need to be sure you have packed correctly. If you need to spend more time reviewing the prior sections, please take it. You will be doing yourself a HUGE favor. It sucks to be in the middle of your epic adventure short on underwear and having forgotten your sunglasses. What does the service section of your guidebook look like? **SERVICE** is the ticket to having access to mentors. If you are cutting any of the previous sections short you will not gain access to the mentors you are looking for. I can guarantee it.

I'm asking you to take some time and be sure you are properly packed for this final stage of the journey. In the *COCONUT WIRELESS LIFE*, adding Mentors to the mix is the equivalent of JET FUEL, so be ready to LAUNCH. Folks, THIS IS A GAME CHANGER.

Do the **HABITS**. Create the **MINDSET**. Be of **SERVICE** and then find your **MENTORS**.

HABITS÷MINDSET÷SERVICE÷MENTORS=CWL

This is the CWL Equation.

Trolley Strap

Wayne Dyer calls it a trolley strap. Being in a relationship with mentors is like having a strap to hold onto attached from above. Picture yourself on a bus, metro, or a train or, I guess, a trolley (dying to know the last time you were on a trolley?).

You get the idea. That strap fastened from the ceiling just keeps you more stable and centered as the bus bumps along. You have something to hold on to. This is the same as a mentor. You MUST be of service to your mentors. It's what allows you the benefit of holding on to the trolley strap. This is no small thing. Mentors can give you a hand up.

Just like a trolley strap.

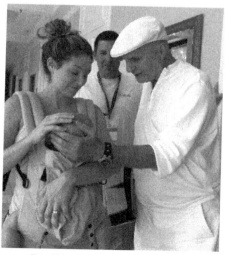

Dr. Wayne W. Dyer, Cooper and me
on Maui Jan 2013

 Check out all the kids books by Dr. Dyer.
Coopers Favorite is *I Am*.

Comfort Zone

You know that popular expression about getting out of your comfort zone? Believe me, it is important to be on purpose about making your way out of your comfort zone. And the key to the magic is about STAYING out of your comfort zone! This is why having mentors is critical to creating your *COCONUT WIRELESS LIFE*. You want to be on purpose about placing people into your life who will keep you out of your comfort zone. This is such an important concept.

Who in your life right now is currently pushing you to grow? To be your most excellent? Your friends, your family? Maybe a little bit. But as you make your way to the end of the guidebook you will see that Mentors have a specific function and purpose in your life. And you will find a far greater return on your efforts when you focus and are on purpose about being of service to your Mentors. Be of service, and stay out of your comfort zone.

Drafting

I am going to share a few thoughts and quotes about how critical it is to seek out Mentors as you progress into your dream life. And like any good protégé, I have drawn from the knowledge and writings of my mentors to sell you this idea. It's going to take effort and it's going to be worth it. BIG TIME!

Life is dynamic. Our world is in constant change. Nobody can afford to delude himself with thinking he has it all figured out, no matter who he is or what experience he can claim.
— CHRIS BRADY and OORWIN WOODWARD
(*Launching a Leadership Revolution*)

Never diminish the power of association.
— KEITH KOCHNER
(Founder of Mentorship Mastery)

The novice's curse is manifested as excessive adornment, silly creativity, weak fundamentals and, ultimately, a marked lack of virtuosity and delayed mastery. If you've ever had the opportunity to be taught by the VERY BEST in any field you've likely been surprised at how simple, how fundamental, how basic the instruction was. The novice's curse afflicts learner and teacher alike.
— GREG GLASSMAN
(Founder of CrossFit)

When I think about my role as a protégé or student with my mentors I recognize that I am using them to help me, prepare and execute my purpose. A mentor is someone you go to for sharpening, honing, to become more effective. It doesn't always feel good, but you know it is good for you.

> The reason a protégé will listen to a mentor is because he believes the mentor can help him get what he wants.
> — CHRIS BRADY and OORWIN WOODWARD
> *(Launching a Leadership Revolution)*

So as you embark on this final section I am encouraging you to reach out to people who want to help you get where you want to go. They are out there.

In the sport of cycling, they call this drafting. In real life, it is the best way to get further faster and with less pain.

The Coconut Wireless. I didn't make this up. You couldn't make this up. It's how Hawai'i works. It's how information and knowledge is passed among people. Humans in networked communities. People on these islands are still in community and connect with each other. It's refreshing. Log off and connect.

Are You My Mentor?

I know you are saying Yes! Drafting, that makes sense. Riding with a group of people all headed the same direction so the work feels easier. Makes a lot of sense, right? So how do you find the select people you want to have as mentors? Don't worry I'm going to help with that. We just keep following the map.

When determining if a particular person truly qualifies as a mentor go thru this list to make sure they are walking the walk in the areas you are focusing on to progress. This is your LIFE we are talking about. BE SELECTIVE. Seek those that you want to learn from and do your due diligence to make sure they are qualified. Mentors are different than friends. Learn the difference.

> A good book contains more wealth than a good bank.
> — ROY L. SMITH

- ✓ "A mentor is someone who cares about the performance of the protégé enough to say what a friend would not. In this regard, a mentor actually goes beyond friendship."

- ✓ "Example is not the main thing in influencing other peoples behavior, it's the ONLY thing."

- ✓ "Find those whom you admire, who are in a position in life you desire to be in, who are living lives in a manner you wish to emulate, and strive to obtain their respect for what you are doing and accomplishing. That is one of the best routes to success."

✓ "What you do speaks so loudly that what you say I cannot hear."

✓ "Mentors rise above mere friendship and provide needed, straight ahead guidance. At times this may be uncomfortable but the price of discomfort with a mentor is much less than the price of discomfort that comes with mistakes in judgment or poor performance in the field."

✓ "Mentors let protégés know that they have the seeds of greatness deep inside, that they do have what it takes to make it."

✓ "Seek the counsel of those who have achieved the goal for which you strive; for in all matters, the words of one who has prospered are far weightier than the words of one who has not."

 All of the concepts above can be found in the book *Launching a Leadership Revolution.* (Such an important book!)

The List

As you are thinking about who some possible mentors could be are you nodding your head and answering yes to the concepts on the last page?

Then you are headed in the right direction.

Just because you want to have someone as a mentor doesn't mean it's going to happen. So have a couple of options. When I did this exercise I had determined there were four people who I wanted to increase my access to. A business/lifestyle mentor. A leadership/cultural mentor and two people whom I wanted mentorship from as professionals working in the field of human behavior/meditation and group processes. Clarify these areas for yourself. Be clear about the areas where you are seeking mentorship so you have a focus for your time together.

Trust your TUG. (I learned this concept from a mentor.) Your TUG is the "gravitational pull around your greatness." Same idea as, "trusting your gut." You will start to get a sense of who your mentors could be, because they are doing things that resonate with you. Pay attention to that feeling. It will be your guide.

Who Made It?

Email them, call them. Ask them to lunch. YOU HAVE NOTHING TO LOSE and EVERYTHING TO GAIN. Most people like to help others, and if you lead with service and are a good student the sky is the limit.

Mentor/Protégé Guidelines and Reminders.

1) You are the expendable one. So it is your responsibility to serve the relationship. Lead with service. True story: I was seeking increased access to one mentor so I basically agreed to be her assistant's assistant. Yep, pretty glamorous. I basically made cold calls to help out Habitat for Humanity because my Mentor was the President of the Board here in Hilo, Hawai'i. Be willing to work to increase your access. You are the expendable one. You are the protégé. Recognize that and act accordingly.

2) A mentor can be your mentor in one area of life or around a specific area like business, family life, leadership, culture, character. The list is endless. When someone is your mentor, it doesn't mean they are your mentor in all areas. Be conscientious about what areas you are seeking mentorship from this person.

3) Take NOTES!!! Are you kidding??? At least write down notes after your time together or tape record the session if you can. They are your MENTORS for God's sake! Some of you are going to be plugging into mentors who have a very high per/hour rate. RECOGNIZE THAT and honor it. Be an excellent student. Excellent students take notes so they can review.

4) It's likely that they don't want you to be around that much. You aren't at their level YET. The time you spend with Mentors is super concentrated. It's not just like hanging with your friends.

So you will need time to sit with, mull over, ponder, review, test, synthesize and act upon the things you are learning from your Mentors. You need the time in between to process. This type of relationship constitutes a Mentor. If you are unsure, it's probably not a Mentor.

 mentorfish.com (Find additional specifics on how to really leverage all that is possible out of a mentoring relationship check out, "Getting Addicted To Your Greatness Bootcamp.")

Ho'ona'auao (gain wisdom)
http://bit.ly/Hoonaauao

This photo is from one of my son's favorite places in Hilo, the Papahānaumokuākea Marine National Monument Discovery Center.
www.papahanaumokuakea.gov

Story Time

Hearing stories from my mentors is how I have absorbed so much that currently informs my life. Time with them (live or recorded) is a chance for me to absorb how they are doing the magic that they do in everyday life. There have been seasons where every day I am listening to something from one of my mentors. Every day. My Ninja Time. This has lead to opportunities to be in working relationships with them as well. This increases the value of my life across the board. I hope these stories from them and from my family add fuel to your journey.

Enjoy the stories.

Share them.

These stories constitute my cellular being.

YAHOOOOOOOOOOOOOOO Cow Lips!

What??? I know. Who knows—I have NO IDEA what this means.

We skied growing up. We went for the first time on a special trip with my dad when we graduated from kindergarten. That is when we learned to ski. Kindergarten graduation one day and then snow plow on the bunny slope the next day. Pretty epic. As we got older my sister Ande and I would shriek, "Yahoo cow lips" as we bombed down the ski slopes of Mammoth Mountain, California. Here is why this story made the cut. My parents put us in situations that allowed us to go totally bonkers and HAVE FUN. To be literally engulfed in FUN. Ande and I would be at the top of the bunny slope, we would tuck into a speed ball with our ski poles tucked into our armpits and sticking out the back like we were downhill Olympic race champions. You gotta let it go once in a while, it's good for you. And my parents creating an environment of fun and passion was so awesome . . . that we just blurted out, "YAHOOO COW LIPS!"

> Don't ask yourself what the world needs. Ask yourself what makes you come alive, and go do that, because what the world needs is people who have come alive.
> — HOWARD THURMAN

 "Yahoo cowlips!" We had no idea—apparently we were yelling about vaginas. Terrific. People with vaginas are special.

Speaking of vaginas (it's where babies come from). And if you like babies or know a mama with a sense of humor check out my next book *Hi'ilani Drop Out*.

Spur You On

Look at the boot with a spur. Think about how that functions. The saying, "spur you on" starts to make sense as you can imagine the motivation of the horse to move when he feels the spur. Mentors do the same thing. They spur you on. I don't mean cheerleading. I mean getting you to work just a little harder, do it better, be more excellent. Here is an example; Julie knew I talked about writing this book. And after not hearing about it for a while she sent me a copy of a book with a similar concept, except—it sucked. I was fired up instantly. I was irritated by the one she had sent. I told her about my reaction when we were walking one day. She said, "I knew you would be. Good. That's why I sent it." My Coconut Wireless writing notes were on the front burner immediately. She had done her job and we both knew it.

That's a mentor.

Protégé note: I am on purpose about being of service to Julie by joining her in exercise and health activities. It's one of the ways I continue to be of service to her. Be active and on purpose about servicing the relationships with your mentors.

- wholelifechallenge.com
- kimpierce.myarbonne.com

Mentor Julie Hugo and me at a Hilo Toastmaster Meeting.
(Summer 2014)

Does It Excite You?

I spent an afternoon at Grif and Noriko's apartment in Hilo, Hawai'i. Their home is refreshing due to lack of clutter. They really only have what they need and nothing else. I had a hard time getting my head around what that meant, and how they got there. I asked Noriko, "What if you get rid of it and then you decide that you do need it?"

Noriko told me that she only keeps what "excites" her. Nothing else. A few times a year Noriko goes through EVERYTHING. Silverware drawer through underwear drawer and asks "Does this excite me?" and if not, she gives it away.

I am now in the habit of giving away more than ever before and feel completely supported by the material possessions that I do have. Our family lives a life that is less bogged down with stuff than ever before. The average person spends A LOT of time thinking about their stuff, buying stuff, managing stuff, returning stuff and driving around to get stuff. Consider having LESS STUFF. It's good for you and the planet. Plus, if it doesn't excite you, give it to someone who will love it more. Remember. We are all connected. This creates good karma FOR SURE.

Give away one thing a day for the next twenty-one days. Even if it's a pair of socks. Create this habit. It will continue to serve you and you will shift your energetic flow towards gifting and abundance.

The hardest thing in the world is to simplify your life.
— YVON CHOUINARD (Founder of Patagonia)

Grif and Noriko Frost

 Do you like Grif's shirt? There are some great stories
behind these images created by Big Island talent.
Check out http://www.akuacreative.com

Steve Jobs

Please tell me you have at least read the book? If not, put it on your list. The way this man would think and then take action completely changed the landscape of multiple industries. Steve Jobs is someone to read about and study. Your mentors don't have to be alive. They can be, but it's not required. Steve Jobs gets his own page because the stories from this man's life continue to inform millions.

Be one of them.

> I've soon come up with 4 juicy-looking colors, in addition to bondi blue, for the imacs. Offering the same computer in 5 colors would of course create huge challenges for manufacturing, inventory and distribution. At most companies, including the old Apple, there would have been studies and meetings to look at the costs and benefits. But when Jobs looked at the colors, he got totally psyched and summoned other executives over to the design studio. "We are going to do all sorts of colors!" He told them excitedly. When they left Ivy looked at his team in amazement. In most places that decision would have taken months. Steve did it in a half hour.[1]

Find **PASSION** in your work. It is so essential to FEEL GOOD and enjoy what you are doing. Jobs liked all the different colored computers . . . so the rest of the world was going to like them too. That simple. That big. That passionate. But also that simple.

 Steve Jobs

---

1. Walter Isaacson, *Steve Jobs* (New York: Simon & Schuster, 2013), 365.

Be Unrealistic

Being realistic is the most common path to mediocrity.
— WILL SMITH

I have made it a point to surf on Monday mornings. I grew up in California where the majority of people sit in traffic on the way to a job they don't love Monday morning. Well, living in paradise increases the heat on your choices because beauty is all around you, beckoning you, so I make it a priority to surf Monday mornings while the rest of America sits in traffic.

On Facebook, I made a post about a Monday morning surf session and got some reverb about being irresponsible and spoiled. It got my attention big time. I didn't like being called those things at all. After some soul searching, I realized that most people are just used to what is REALISTIC. Surfing Monday mornings isn't realistic. But I'm not seeking a realistic, mediocre life. I am seeking a bad ass, ridiculously fun, built around service and greatness kind of life. So I keep surfing Monday mornings. After that soul searching, I made it a point to make sure there is fun and passion in my day every day. I also started to make lists of my tasks in the day so I could see the progression. Here is an example of the progression.

Fall 2006, wake up to an alarm, drive to the office, turn on the computer and stare out the window wishing I could be outside. Do my work, eat my lunch, sit in meetings that don't accomplish much of anything, finish work and think about exercising, chose not to exercise because a day without passion is exhausting, make dinner, watch TV, go to bed. Repeat 5x a week FOREVER unless something changes.

Winter 2012, wake up to alarm so I can sneak out of house before my son wakes up, surfboard in car, paddle into the line up, sit with friends and whales, grab coffee, work from home office on the three most essential tasks to complete that day, have lunch, be of service to a mentor, get a massage, spend late afternoon with son and husband in the yard, exercise because it feels good, make a dinner that is simple and nourishing, read and write. REPEAT. YES, PLEASE!

It's not about perfection. It's about Progression.
— UNKNOWN

Being realistic doesn't actually serve you.

 The Slight Edge by Jeff Olsen. (Yes I know it's in here twice. It's that important.)

 Charlie Rose Interview with Will Smith. Air Date 3/13/2002
http://bit.ly/WSmithCWL

Flow

In High School, some of my friends used to call my dad "Ron Dogg."

Yep, double G, like a gangster.

Don't ask, it would be impossible to explain.

Sometimes Ron Dogg would say, "When you're hot, you're hot."

So if we got out of the parking lot quickly and not caught in traffic, or when plans laid out just the way he wanted, when it all just worked, my dad would say to my sister and me, "Girls, when you're hot you're hot." It was his way of gloating.

What I realize now is that these were small examples of my dad experiencing FLOW.

FLOW is what happens when you make it a habit of doing things that you love and also doing the tasks that you need to do, well. When these two phenomena collide; you experience FLOW. There is potential for FLOW in everything. We all have different passions. Your passion is what creates your *COCONUT WIRELESS LIFE*. There is flow in writing, cooking, surfing, ANYTHING that you are passionate about. You will know it is happening because what you are doing feels effortless and brilliant. You could do it all day.

There was a big chunk of time growing up where I played a lot of soccer. I mean AYSO on steroids. Year-round, all the time for a lot of years in a row. I wasn't necessarily the best, but there came a time that I could do things that were hard and make it look easy. I LOVED playing soccer. I was in FLOW. It was effortless and fun. It was directly linked to my willingness to practice even when it wasn't quite as *flowy*.

Most things are like that. Do the work. Be consistent about the work and the fun comes.

Want to majorly increase your FLOW? Watch *The Secret*. I watched it 30 times in 90 days. Don't judge. What the hell do you watch 30x in 90 days? The news? Some bitchy housewives show? Great choice.

Increase your FLOW.

 Watch *The Secret* repeatedly

 Speaking of FLOW, local people totally get the concept of FLOW better than most. Check out this Art FLOW:

- extremeexposure.com
- clarklittlephotography.com

Threshold Training

At this point who hasn't heard of CrossFit? Look it up. For the sake of jumping through hoops, getting certificates and increasing my fundamentals I became a Level 1 Certified trainer in CrossFit.

This is where I learned about THRESHOLD TRAINING.

Here is it. Drum roll, please.

Make it harder. Then make it perfect. Then make it harder. Then make it perfect . . . over and over and over again. This leads to a state of virtuosity. (Virtuosity is doing the common uncommonly well.)

You appear to be on another level. And this is true for your physical being, spiritual being and quality of life. Make it hard, practice a lot, make it perfect, then make it harder again.

This is what humans are capable of.

 crossfit.com

 Where I CrossFit and yoga, Hilo Health Cooperative:
www.hilohealth.coop
(Hawai'i's first cooperative fitness center.)

Hot Under the Collar

Keeping service at the foundation of your relationships to your mentors will allow you to continue to have access to them. The more time you have with a mentor, the more you can learn. This increases the depth and dimension of the learning curve incredibly quickly. I have a mentor named Dr. Lynn Puana. She is a top ranked consultant in the same business as me. It's why she is a Mentor for me. I attended a training that Lynn was hosting and a new consultant asked her if she had ever been turned down or gotten a rejection in her business. Now, Lynn is stunning, successful, smart, and fun to be around. A person who lives life full out and with style. This question about rejection was a good one to ask because people like Lynn appear to be above rejection. As Lynn was telling the new consultant that yes indeed, she has faced rejection, she gave specifics about the story. As the story went on Lynn literally got hot under the collar. Her neck got red and blotchy, she got a little flustered. It was terrific. It was terrific because it's a reminder that our Mentors are HUMAN. The journey never ends. No matter your accomplishments in life you still get hot under the collar. And isn't that refreshing? Mentors are not idols. A mentor is a human you are learning from.

 For a real-deal glimpse of these incredible islands by someone born and raised here check out The *Red-headed Hawaiian* by Chris McKinney and Rudy Puana M.D. (Lynn's husband)

O.P.D.

This is a snapshot of life growing up in my family.

O.P.D. This stands for Opportunity for Personal Development.

Clawing a crumbling dirt ledge and looking down the other side as the trail drops into the ocean. My Mom was sweating it and we could tell.

I said, "Look Mom, an O.P.D!"

I believe her response was, "FUCK THE O.P.D!" My sister and I were howling laughing because our mom said the F word. Needless to say, the expression stuck around.

When you find yourself in an uncomfortable situation, remember O.P.D. That is it. It's just a new or uncomfortable situation. This is actually a good thing. It stretches you to think about something differently, try something new in your body and test the waters outside your comfort zone. My mom had zero interest in testing the ocean water that day . . . but she has a cellular memory of her O.P.D.

This event left such an impression on our family that for my Mom's birthday she had O.P.D shirts made for us. Ridiculous I know, but the good kind of ridiculous.

There is a Canadian athletic company called lululemon athletica. (Yes, some people live under a rock, or on a rock in the middle of the ocean.) LuluLemon has these fancy bags you get when you purchase something. One of the bags says, "do something every day that scares you." So my challenge to you is . . . DO IT.

Don't buy the $50 sports bra and just look the part. Go out there, do it, find your ledge and bring on the O.P.D.

Some choices for O.P.D

✓ Do a handstand against a wall, or sit in a chair and put your head between your knees. It's good to be upside down.

✓ Try oil pulling to clean your teeth, seems wacky, but it's awesome. Google it.

✓ Cook something way out of the ordinary.

✓ Try a Zumba class, yoga or CrossFit tomorrow.

✓ Turn off the TV and read.

✓ Write a note to a friend or write a note to an enemy.

✓ Be extra nice to a stranger.

✓ Help a mentor.

✓ Don't get out of bed until you are thankful that you CAN get out of bed.

✓ Make a list of 5 things you are thankful for.

✓ Listen more, then think, then think again, then talk.

✓ Run or walk an extra mile.

✓ Swim in the ocean.

Wrapping It Up: What's Important NEXT?

This became my mantra after my son was born. The spiritual heat of parenthood burns away the excess fat and waste in all your habits. There is no more dilly-dallying in the bathroom to pluck your eyebrows, or what I call "housing about" where you just put things away and move around piles. (I know you do this.) 😎

I made the decision before Cooper was born that he was going to blossom my life. I was going to be an awesome parent AND a capable person. Not a mom who scraps everything and becomes flaky, disoriented and unfocused in the name of raising children. By asking yourself "What's important next," you will accelerate your ability to determine what actually matters and in what order. In the first months of motherhood, I hardly knew which way was north due to sleep deprivation and the newness of it all. But I could always manage to ask myself "What's important next" and then do just that task. Just that task. It doesn't have to be fancy, it just has to be done. We live in a world with too many options. You put your child down for a nap and the options of things to do are so endless that you can easily just do NONE OF THEM. This question gives you a chance to determine the single right action to do next. When you complete it, ask yourself again, then again, then take a nap. Life can be totally nuts. Plan for that and just ask yourself "What's important next?"

As we wrap up our time together in *COCONUT WIRELESS LIFE*, here is what's important next: We are going to talk about **LOVE**, **COURAGE** and making your *COCONUT WIRELESS LIFE* **MOVE**.

Doodle space below to nurture your great adventures!

Hugs and High Five.

Love

Love. It certainly fits in here somewhere. In this whole big picture of life, it sure seems that it is fairly close to the center. Take it for all it's worth. DEFAULT TO LOVE. Here are some thoughts from a woman who has built a life and political platform centered on LOVE.

Love takes more than crystals and rainbows, it takes discipline and practice. It's not just a sweet sentiment from a Hallmark card. It is a radical commitment to a different way of being, a mental response to life that is completely at odds with the thinking of the world.
— MARIANNE WILLIAMSON

Personal power emanates from someone who takes life seriously. The universe takes us as seriously as we take it. There is no greater seriousness than the full appreciation of the power and importance of LOVE. Miracles flow from the recognition that LOVE is the purpose of our careers.
— MARIANNE WILLIAMSON

Can you imagine writing that on your resume?! Experience: LOVE. Career goals: LOVE. Ph.D. in LOVE. Seeking employment related to LOVE. SOUNDS CRAZY huh? I KNOW! But I believe that when you boil it all down this is where it MUST begin. Today we are so smart, so capable and so unfriendly to each other it is FUCKING UP EVERYTHING. Countries hate each other, we as humans have an averaged chronic disregard for mother nature and very few people even think about love at all. I have no idea how we got to this state. When is the last time you contemplated your relationship with LOVE?

I began to realize that taking love seriously would be a complete transformation of my thinking.
— MARIANNE WILLIAMSON

If I want to know GOD I must LOVE MYSELF.
— NAHKO and MEDICINE FOR THE PEOPLE

you're gonna get to love yourself. I'm not talking about conceit. I'm talking about a healthy respect for yourself.
— BOB PROCTOR

There is undeniable root to fruit connection between our heart and our behavior. People and situations do not determine our behavior; they provide the occasion where our behavior reveals our hearts. Lasting change always takes place thru the pathways of the heart.
— PAUL DAVID TRIPP

- *A Return to Love* by Marianne Williamson
- *Change We Must* by Nana Veary

"Aloha Ke Akua" by Nahko and Medicine for the People
I am a miracle made up of particles.

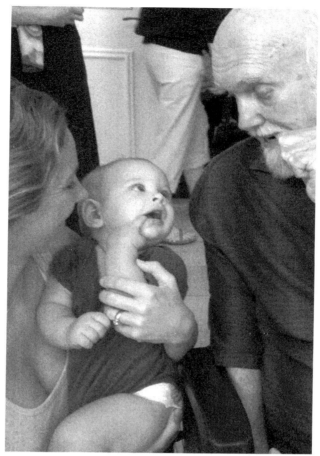

Ram Dass, my son and me.
(They were speaking the same language without words.)

 ramdass.org

Courage

When I think about courage, I think about a lion ROARING. Being brave and courageous. At times, courage comes in those silent moments when you just begin again. Courage is a choice. It's a decision to keep participating in life as fully as you can humanly muster. Even on days when a ROAR is more like a squeak from a kitty cat. Because sometimes courage is like that too.

I think that so often we hesitate, we hesitate to smile, to share, to risk connection, to ask for what we want, to stay in tune with our purpose. We make up stories that we aren't smart enough, good enough, fill in the blank enough and then we talk ourselves out of it before we ever began. This is big, big, big bummers. Because it builds up over a lifetime. And you my friend, are destined to do something important in this life.

So focus on courage. Just focus on making those seemingly small but important choices. Let your heart be your guide. Sometimes people think they need "more self-confidence" before they begin something. Rarely is this true, we need more courage.

Thanks for being on this CWL with me. Now for our final lesson: making it MOVE.

X Marks The Spot — Now MOVE

Okay guys, this is it. You have absorbed stories from my Mentors and my family, now it's time to MOVE. There is no such thing as coincidence. You got this book because the planet wanted you to have this book and you attracted it to yourself. I hope you know that in your mind and feel that in your heart. So be in action. MAKE IT MOVE. Your *COCONUT WIRELESS LIFE* is available. Move into it and tell someone else what you are up to! With privilege comes great responsibility.

We live on a globe that is suffering. Nature is suffering, people are suffering. Perhaps now more than every before. We (INCLUDING ME) have been greedy, misguided and focused on things that do not serve our highest calling. I'm going to step off my soap box and just say that you have everything you need in you already. You have lessons and people around you to make a positive impact in your corner of this interconnected globe. THIS IS YOUR *COCONUT WIRELESS LIFE*. So make it MOVE. Share it.

Be a life raft. Be a life raft in the way that you live your life. Others will grab on. They will float and extend that offering to others. It's not about an ideology or religion, it's about HUMANS BEING CONNECTED.

> People who profoundly achieve aren't necessarily people who do so much; they're people around whom things get done. Mahatma Gandhi and President Kennedy were both examples of this. Their greatest achievement lay in all the energy they stirred in other people, the invisible forces they unleashed around them. By touching their own depths, they touched the depths within others.
> — MARIANNE WILLIAMSON

in this existence, I'll stay persistent, and I'll make a difference . . .
— NAHKO and MEDICINE FOR THE PEOPLE

The most glorious human potential—our capacity to change.
— MARIANNE WILLIAMSON

MAKE IT MOVE!

I LOVE YOU,

And thanks for being on the Journey of the
COCONUT WIRELESS LIFE
Alooooooooooooooooha!

 Go float in water. Just float. Lean back, be vulnerable and float.

 Eaarth by Bill McKibben

 vice.com (my favorite news source)

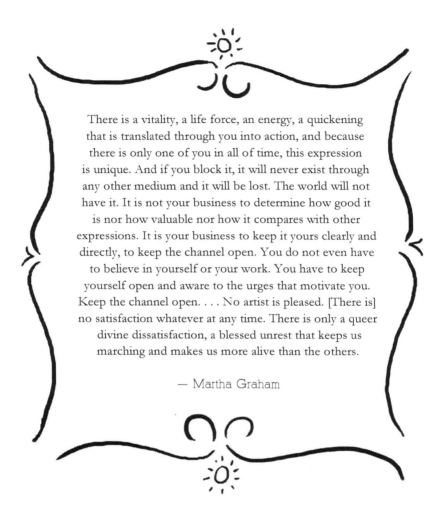

There is a vitality, a life force, an energy, a quickening that is translated through you into action, and because there is only one of you in all of time, this expression is unique. And if you block it, it will never exist through any other medium and it will be lost. The world will not have it. It is not your business to determine how good it is nor how valuable nor how it compares with other expressions. It is your business to keep it yours clearly and directly, to keep the channel open. You do not even have to believe in yourself or your work. You have to keep yourself open and aware to the urges that motivate you. Keep the channel open. . . . No artist is pleased. [There is] no satisfaction whatever at any time. There is only a queer divine dissatisfaction, a blessed unrest that keeps us marching and makes us more alive than the others.

— Martha Graham

60408515R00062

Made in the USA
Charleston, SC
25 August 2016